Seán Street has published six collections of poetry, the most recent being *Radio and Other Poems*. He has worked in radio as a writer, producer and presenter for more than thirty years and his work is frequently to be heard on BBC Radios 3 and 4. His prose includes a number of texts on radio history, a well as writings on Gerard Manley Hopkins and The Dymock Poets. Seán Street is Professor of Radio in the Bournemouth Media School at Bournemouth University.

RADIO WAVES

Poems Celebrating the Wireless

Compiled by Seán Street

PREFACE BY JENNY ABRAMSKY

ENITHARMON PRESS

For Jo, Jemma and Zoë
and in memory of David Gascoyne

First published in 2004
by the Enitharmon Press
26B Caversham Road
London NW5 2DU

www.enitharmon.co.uk

Distributed in the UK by
Central Books
99 Wallis Road
London E9 5LN

Distributed in the USA and Canada
by Dufour Editions Inc.
PO Box 7, Chester Springs
PA 19425, USA

ISBN 1 900564 39 4

Enitharmon Press gratefully acknowledges the
financial support of Arts Council England, London.

British Library Cataloguing-in-Publication Data.
A catalogue record for this book is available
from the British Library.

Typeset in Bembo by Servis Filmsetting Ltd, Manchester
and printed in England by
Antony Rowe Ltd.

CONTENTS

Epilogue

PREFACE

Radio Waves is like the best programme ideas – original, engaging, yet so simple it's hard to believe no one has thought of it before. A glance down the list of contributors to Seán Street's anthology reveals the range of the medium's appeal, from Norman Long's 1930s variety act to the daunting intellect of Geoffrey Hill, Philip Larkin, W. H. Auden, Seamus Heaney, Carol Ann Duffy, Gillian Clarke; indeed, most of the best-known poets of the last fifty years have written radio poems.

It is interesting that while reading such a wide variety of poets common themes emerge. Poets love lists and find the names of sea areas of the Shipping Forecast and radio stations themselves irresistible. For several, radio is strongly evocative and the way it – the set itself as well as what comes out - lingers in the memory belies the essentially ephemeral nature of the medium. Then there is reaction to what is heard and what this signifies, leading to the unlikely linking of D. H. Lawrence with the Western Brothers. Some poets are disconcerted as well as fascinated, and concerned for language itself when it is broadcast. Several are amazed by the simple power of radio, the fact of hearing an event elsewhere and the human implications of this. So Philip Larkin in 'Broadcast' is desperate to pick out in the applause the clapping, 'tiny in all that air', of the individual who matters to him.

Seán Street is exactly the person to explore the wealth of work resulting from radio listening. He is a radio scholar teaching at Bournemouth University, where he became Britain's first Professor of Radio. But his interest is by no means solely academic. He creates radio, making entertaining and innovative programmes for the BBC's national networks. And he is a poet who has published six collections, the most recent being *Radio*, taking its title from a sequence inspired by Radio 4. These poems were broadcast throughout National Poetry

Day in 1998, beginning a tradition of the network marking National Poetry Day with specially commissioned pieces for radio.

Radio Waves begins like a radio programme (before digital) with a hiss in the opening poem by Michael Symmons Roberts. It ends with a poem by Charles Tomlinson about recording, once the programme is finished, some ambience, some silence. And like all good programmes, when *Radio Waves* concludes, it leaves you hungry for more.

JENNY ABRAMSKY
Director of Radio and Music, BBC

INTRODUCTION

What are the wild waves saying
Sister, the whole day long,
That ever amid our playing
I hear but their low lone song?

Joseph Edwards Carpenter's words date from long before the advent of radio. Nevertheless, the power of radio waves – like the sea – has an elemental quality about it which evoked an almost superstitious awe amongst early listeners. Indeed, the medium continues to invade our minds and hearts through its ability to speak directly to us, and so often to do so while we are engaged in another activity – part of its uniqueness. From its earliest days, poets of all kinds have chosen it either to write FOR or to write ABOUT. In December 1927 *Radio Times* published a page of poetry about radio with the following introduction:

> It is not a strange thing that men have made poems about Broadcasting, for the new magic, which pours the music of the concert room into the stillness of the cottage and brings the song of nightingales into the heart of Town, is of the very stuff of poetry.

Radio Times – particularly in its pre-war years – carried on an honourable tradition of commissioning poems. Even more recently the journal had its own poet in residence, Roger Woddis, who, for a number of years, wrote a verse commentary on a current programme or theme. Alfred Noyes's 'The Dane Tree', written to celebrate the opening of the giant Daventry transmitter in 1925, is one example of this policy which illustrates the mystical power of the invisible medium, and for many years early wireless enthusiasts would talk of 'searching the ether' for distant signals. John Reith, the British

Broadcasting Company's General Manager, later to become the first Director General of the British Broadcasting Corporation, himself wrote of this strange power in his 1924 autobiography, *Broadcast Over Britain*:

> When we attempt to deal with ether we are immediately involved in the twilight shades of the borderland; darkness presses in on all sides, and the intensity of the darkness is increased by the illuminations which here and there are shed, as the investigators, candle in hand and advancing step by step, peer into the illimitable unknown.

For the early pioneers radio was indeed a sacred cause, tapping into intangible forces which, through their scientific reality, provided a key for a door into another, unseen world. Time and again in the early writings about radio, this sense of awe shows itself. It is no coincidence that some of the finest radio producers, including Louis MacNeice, George MacBeth, Paul Muldoon, Julian May and Michael Symmons Roberts have also been poets. Radio and poetry have a lot in common; both can supply clues without telling us how to interpret. Radio, like poetry, strikes matches in the mind.

Radio is a personal medium; sound is so often memory, and a theme within the book is that of recollection, sometimes manifesting itself as nostalgia, often as the remembrance of a door opening, a seminal moment. Sound can transport us to another time and place when we least expect it, because of the subliminal nature of a voice or voices murmuring in our ear. People often even become attached to the object itself – the old battered set that has sat in the kitchen for years, or on a bedside table; at the turn of the century the statistics told us that the average number of radios per British home was six. Some of those sets will have been around for many years, their very shape and appearance a part of the fabric of lives, switched on day after day without thinking, as one turns on a light. I cannot think of any other electronic device capable of exciting affection in its own right, certainly not a television set or a computer. Nor - personally - can I imagine TV as an inspiration for the writing of poetry.

One of the great qualities of 'the wireless' is its endless ability to reinvent itself; another is the power to talk to millions and to one person simultaneously. It is a power which has made it dangerous as well as comforting over the years. Not yet at its centenary, it is, together with the Internet, one of the most significant communications creations of the last one hundred years. There might be those who would argue the case for television, but television would not have happened had radio not happened first. The various aspects of radio, its many voices and songs, are celebrated in this collection, as are some of the darker truths of the medium, and the power of its content to anger, irritate and terrify. As with all technology, there is always the potential for abuse.

The anthology is deliberately eclectic, like radio in its early days. Reith's idea of good listening was serendipity, the potential for the medium to surprise from one programme to another. In the modern broadcasting world, with its branding and generic streaming, there is less opportunity for this, but it can still happen. So here you will find the words of David Gascoyne a few pages away from the comedian Ronald Frankau (David would have liked that); elsewhere Brecht speaks of the power of sound to pour dogma and hate into his ear, while Gavin Ewart celebrates *Test Match Special*, and Stella Davis sings in praise of *The Archers*. Radio has been the inspiration for much finely crafted poetry by leading writers, while at the same time *Radio Times, Punch* and other journals have given space to simple verses by listeners, short reflections expressing some emotion or another provoked by the act of listening, or - in the early days - of actually *creating* the means of listening through the building of the family radio. The ingenuity of listeners in parodying well-known writers and styles while wrestling with the technology of the 1920s produced some amusing references. Although it is not a poem, it is worth quoting R. M. Freeman's evocation of 'Samuel Pepys, Listener':

May 5. My wife and I listening-in this night, but the heering indifferent; so to fiddle with the buttons, my wife in her busy way telling me I am like only to make bad worse by my fiddling. And, as the devil will have it, in the midst of my fiddling, out goes one of the valves, through a fused wire. Whereat my wife, like the fool she is, do lay all to me rather than to the fused wire, saying 'There, Samuel, what did I tell you?' and other taunting things; so that how I did keep my hands off her, God knows.

A. J. Campbell, with apologies to Kipling, picked up the theme:

If you can make a choice when all about you
Are praising 'dynes' and 'supers', 'Reinartz' too;
If you can estimate what it will cost you
To build a set for Rome or Timbuctoo:
If you can listen nor be tired by listening
To friends' romance of what their circuits do,
And in the end settle yourself to making
The set you're keen on (less a valve or two) . . .

One of the legion of *Radio Times*'s anonymous scribes of the 1930s wrote, in 'The Listeners':

'Is there anything good?' said the Listener,
Turning on the Regional wave.
And his friend in the silence waited, waited
For the noise that the sound-box gave.
And a song flew up out of the wireless
Over the listener's head,
And he turned the little knob a second time:
'I don't want *that*' he said.

Nor did John Masefield escape the parodying pen of a listener from Hounslow, in 'BBC Fever':

I must part with ten bob again for licensing time is nigh –
And all I ask is a good set, and a knob to tune her by,
And a merry song for a man to sing, and a lovely girl to sigh for,
And a Middleton talk, and This Week's Sport is what I cry for.

I have tried to identify in this book the moods and genres of the medium, from the invisible magic of its signal and its metaphor for communication between human beings, through music and talk radio, including news. The weather is represented too; it is interesting to see what an inspiration the Shipping Forecast has been - a poem in itself after all. The car remains one of the great places to listen of course; how many of us have arrived at our destination before the programme has finished, and sought to create strategies for staying in the car in order to hear the end? All of which leads us to the experience of listening itself, and the crucial role of the audience in what is after all a mutual act of creation, maker and tuner-in, actively engaged in an experience shaped by the imagination. Our final transmission has Charles Tomlinson in the studio, sitting patiently while the Studio Manager on the other side of the glass records ambience. As he does so, the moment recalls the silence out of which all radio grows – the moment before the first sound, a moment of infinite possibility, like the moment before Marconi's first transmitted Morse Code 'S' of May 1897, remembered by Michael Symmons Roberts in the Prologue to this collection. Another metaphor for the human condition perhaps, because growing out of the invisible stillness of ether, radio returns finally to vanish there. Even if its signals continue to exist somewhere beyond our hearing, 'wireless always ends in silence.'

SEÁN STREET

PROLOGUE

MICHAEL SYMMONS ROBERTS
(b. 1963)

Wireless

(In May 1897, Marconi sent the first radio message across water, from Lavernock in South Wales, to Flat Holm in the Bristol Channel. The message was the letter 'S')

'S', hiss, primal sound, default letter
from which all speech, music, books were born,
dot-dot-dot, morse for white noise.
The first trip radio made over water
carried as its luggage 'S'; waves across waves
it told the sea a story in its own voice,
a tale of water on a shingle beach.

★

In hyperspaces between stations,
radio reverts to sibilance, to 'S',
the universal broadcast of a plural.
Maybe Marconi was weaned on a word
made to be whispered – *sarsaparilla* –
dark juice of underground forced up
on a breath between palate and tongue.

★

'S' in morse without 'O' 'S'. Save, just
save – he was too uncertain of his soul.
Does radio have a half-life, weakening
as it loops and loops the world?
Somewhere in a dripping cave where wireless
goes to die, Marconi's 'S' curls like a paper
message washed out of its bottle.

16

Obsolete distress calls dumped by radio
waves in rock pools glow like ripe
cherry anemones. I fished some out
and held against my ear the faded maydays,
tragic as Titanic luggage, unpacked
now by scientists, silk and lace falling
from their folds like shimmering spirits.

★

White roses as sensitive as crystal sets,
planted at the end of each row of vines.
If there's sickness in the air, roses will
fall first, and precious champagne grapes
are sprayed and netted. So it was
with the earliest receivers.
They would catch a voice and die with it.

★

Marconi's voice: *sarsaparilla was my first,*
waterglass my last, but I will keep
one more 'S' back, so when my tomb
is unsealed I will hiss
through parchment lips and then my face,
my origami death mask,
will be shocked to dust by open air.

★

Wildtrack – radio with no voices, music,
codes, the sound of unmarked canvas.
At the end of each recording, thirty seconds'
nothing, a shared stillness. Actors,
audiences, engineers all honour it
because the dumb deserve a hearing,
and wireless always ends in silence.

SIGNALS

ALFRED NOYES
(1880–1958)

The Dane Tree

*(Written for the official opening of the Daventry Transmitting
Station, 1925, and broadcast during the inaugural ceremony)*

Daventry calling . . . Dark and still
The dead men sleep, at the foot of the hill.

The dark tree, set on the height by the Dane
Stands like a sentry over the slain.

Bowing his head above their tomb
Till the trumpet rends the seals of doom.

Earth has forgotten their ancient wars,
But the lone tree rises against the stars,

Whispering, *'Here in my heart I keep
Mysteries, deep as the world is deep.'*

*'Deeper far than the world ye know
Is the world through which my voices go . . .'*

Daventry calling . . . Wind and rain
Against my voices fight in vain.

The world through which my messages fare
Is not of the earth, and not of the air.

When the black hurricane rides without,
My least melodies quell its shout.

My mirth and music, jest and song,
Shall through the very thunders throng.

You shall hear their lightest tone
Stealing through your walls of stone;

Till your loneliest valleys hear
The far cathedral's whispered prayer,

And thoughts that speed the world's desire
Strike to your heart beside your fire;

And the mind of half the world
Is in each little house unfurled.

Till Time and Space are a dwindling dream,
And my true kingdoms round you gleam;

And ye discern the thing ye crave –
That I do deeper than the grave;

I, the sentinel; I, the tree,
Who bind all worlds in unity,

So that, sitting around your hearth,
Ye are at one with all on earth.

Daventry calling: memory, love,
The graves beneath, and the stars above.

Even in my laughter you shall hear
The Power to whom the far is near.

All are in one circle bound,
And all that ever was lost is found.

Daventry calling . . . Daventry calling . . .
Daventry calling . . . Dark and still
The tree of memory stands like a sentry . . .
Over the graves on the silent hill.

CHARLES BENNETT
(b. 1954)

The Drowned Radio

Recovered by fisherman who saw
a chest of gold below them

its casing warped like ribs of carp
its needle stuck on Hilversum

this silted brain is working
perfectly still.

Stand by the water for a while
as a swan swims once round the island –

soon you'll become attuned
to the soft conversation of clouds

and notice how a minnow's heart
ticks with the drizzle of static.

JAMES PRIORY
(b. 1973)

Emma and the Radio

You find a box beneath the bed
And somehow switch it into life,
Then gently tease a metal thread
Until it flowers above your head,
Bristling at the knowingness of your fingers.
Strangely in-tune with an out-of-tune radio
You joyride the dials,
Freewheel the frequencies,
Detonating syllables like someone shouting in their sleep.
You slide along sliproads of whispers,
Spaces between stations
Which hiss like traffic in rain,
Or pebbles rattling in the lungs of a river.
And then you're on your feet again.
Padding away in pyjamas
To raid your sister's room,
You leave the buzzing box behind,
Deaf to its persistent *sssh*

DESMOND GRAHAM
(b. 1940)

The Wireless

(for Seán Street)

Elgar started it
and Elgar finished it,
the episode my father and I
wallowed in and I feared
brought terror round the corner
twice a week, 'Great Expectations',
the actors' names unknown then
to me and now;

the novel later read
with the pictures by Cruikshank
or Phiz judged not by pages
and stories beside them
but by shapes and shadows
decorating the whole room
without changing the wallpaper,
stoking the fire;

the wireless carried its voices
like cloud delivering people
from all over London,
brought the whole east coast
of England, its tides, its fog
and foghorns, up the cold staircase
onto the landing and through
all night to my bed.

JONATHAN WONHAM
(b. 1965)

Emergency Services

I'd lie there with a book, until the lights went out.
That's when his radio came on, its aerial
taped to the bed frame, emergency services
pouring their sweet nothings in his ear.

Out of the crackling, he'd give us all the facts:
House aflame. Requesting ambulance and tenders . . .
Every incident he logged, and we, at first,
were interested in him, his excited reports.

But that was the tireless world of work
and soon we saw the underlying pattern
in all those gorse fires, chimney fires
and mangled wrecks down country roads.

We gave up caring. Little Greg resumed
his eulogies of cowboy boots and silk kerchiefs
and I turned my face to the great south window
where stars burned freely in the vast, untended night.

ETHAN GILSDORF
(b. 1966)

Away from Us

Away from the window
where I will never know
earth, birds swoop
and rehearse with cars
for the spring show.
Songs and radios mix
and make each other known.

Today the buds emit
weak signals, confused
by the unresolved thermometer
night after night. Flowers meet,
close shop, iris in their lips
and decide to hold out
for a better offer.

In the neighbourhoods,
when spring finally arrives
from hulls of clouds,
flattered and fuchsia scented,
it sits up and performs
yellow and red
from vases and beds.

But in a wooded place
the inclined fiddlehead
has its own reasons
for not showing up.
In its spiral away from us
are the thousand looks it never gets.

ANON.

Wireless at Night

Tall as a village spire
A slender fir-tree set upon the hill
Carries the news – or Chopin – at your will
Along the fine-drawn wire.
Aerial and telephone,
Batteries, valves (so little for so much),
And half of Europe answers to your touch,
Whispers to you alone.

The dogs of Paris bark
For us . . . within a voice comes through:
'Bonsoir, Mesdames, Messieurs' I hear it say,
'L'audition de ce soir est terminée.'
Monsieur, good-night to you.

Punch, 1924

28

GILLIAN CLARKE
(b. 1937)

On Air

Tools of my father's art: old radios
of fretted wood and bakelite.
In a sanctum of shot-silk curtained window
crystal or valve lurked in its holy light.

I turned the knob. The needle wavered on
through crackling distances, Paris, Luxembourg, Hilversum,
past the call-sign of some distant station,
a lonely lightship where infinity scrambles to a hum

the Chinese whispers of a jabbering world.
And now, by transistor and satellite we hear
Beethoven in Berlin sooner than if we were there
on air-waves the speed of light. And when the wall crumbled

we heard the first stone fall before they could.
We watch storms darken the map from the crow's nest
of the weather satellite, hear the swallow's foot
on the wind's telegraph before she comes to rest,

the sun dried to a pellet in her throat.
Still lodged at the wingfeather's bloodroot
a grain of desert sand,
and on my car a veil of strange red dust.

ALAN BROWNJOHN
(b. 1931)

September 1939

I walked into the garden afterwards:

Away up there the soft silver elephants

                               hovered   peculiarly

The wireless had gone over to
A band . . . Or a short feature?
Whichever, I didn't listen.

My mother listened on, half-listened on,
And was thinking, as she watched me from the window.
She told me that.

There was no one in the gardens on either side,
And I too thought: *It will be different now.*

The elephants' noses wrinkled in the breeze.

MUSIC RADIO

W. W. GIBSON
(1878–1962)

Music Stole In

Music stole in; and all the idle chatter
Of gossip tongues was stilled; and for an hour
Our hearts were held by the ethereal power
Forgetful of the long day's fret and clatter.

No longer in a narrow track of duty
Each life moved dully in its little round:
Released from servitude by magic sound,
Our hearts were one with the eternal beauty.

PHILIP LARKIN
(1922–85)

Broadcast

Giant whispering and coughing from
Vast Sunday-full and organ-frowned-on spaces
Precede a sudden scuttle on the drum,
'The Queen', and huge resettling. Then begins
A snivel on the violins:
I think of your face among all those faces,

Beautiful and devout before
Cascades of monumental slithering,
One of your gloves unnoticed on the floor
Beside those new, slightly-outmoded shoes.
Here it goes quickly dark. I lose
All but the outline of the still and withering

Leaves on half-emptied trees. Behind
The glowing wavebands, rabid storms of chording
By being distant overpower my mind
All the more shamelessly, their cut-off shout
Leaving me desperate to pick out
Your hands, tiny in all that air, applauding.

Radio 3

Look, Bach, I'm sorry to switch you off,
But only God is allowed to go on being
Right all the time in detail and in sum
And then say it all twice, back to front,
Upside down and get it right again.
Once for all, you are totally absolutely
Endlessly right. You are fundamentally
Finally right.
Now will you please shut up.

BRIAN LEVISON
(b. 1941)

Eighth Symphony Interruptus

'Open the door!' you order,
And then – 'a drink of water!'
Obedient to yet another wish
I bend for a breathy goodnight kiss.

Upstairs on the radio,
Bruckner's great adagio
In chordal magnificence draws near
The climax I was waiting to hear.

I hurry along the hall,
Leap stairs. Halfway up you call –
Your forte voice louder than Bruckner's –
'Daddy, the door, the door!' Your five years

Will not be denied, but then
Neither would I deny them.
You are my music, little daughter,
More marvellous than Mozart, Mahler.

NORMAN LONG

From: *We Can't Let you Broadcast That*

(Popular song lyric, 1933)

Now the BBC once wrote to me and said 'Dear Norman Long,
We thought you'd like to face the mike with your piano, smile and
    song,
So will you bring your repertoire along for us to see,
To go over it with a pencil of the blue variety.'

So I looked my list of songs up, to the studio I flew,
I said here's a nice song called *Violets*, 'Oh,' they said 'that's much
    too blue',
I said 'Is Robin Adair alright?' They said 'Robin Add-Hair, my hat,
Just think of the bald-headed men you'll upset, we can't let you
    broadcast that.'

So I looked my list of songs up, to please the listening throng,
I said, 'Now here's a good one, *The Volga Boatman's Song.*'
But they hated vulgar boatmen and discouraged vulgar chat,
'And songs about loose sailors are barred, we can't let you broadcast
    that.'

So I looked my list of songs up and found an army one,
'*There's Something About a Soldier*,' but they said 'That can't be done,
There's Something About a Soldier would get over nice and pat
To a sergeant's wife with fourteen kids, we can't let you broadcast
    that.'

So I looked my list of songs up, I was getting fed up to the roots,
I said 'Here's a good song by Kipling, a military song called *Boots.*'
They said 'My dear good fellow, do you realise where you're at?
You're advertising a chemistry firm, we can't let you broadcast that.'

So I packed my list of songs up; I said 'Hang it, I won't sing,
I can do some adagio dancing, or a spot of conjuring,
Trick cycling, walk the tight-rope, I'm a darn good acrobat.'
I'd love to tell you what they said – but I can't even record that.

KEITH BENNETT

99.9 FM Radio Nostalgia

Ah, but when I was young there was this hiss
that burnt the bed sheets close to my lips
as Luxembourg ran out of steam again and slipped
once more into a state of bliss.
The knowledge that what should have been on show
was missing in the channel, or above it, was enough
to keep me mouthing out the words until the gruff
hiss resolved itself into the faint strains of a song I let grow
back into the solid state sound, for I was young
and this was radio at the cutting edge of music
and the rhythmic motion of my bed was innocence.
This was Americana in a radio bell that had to be rung
louder than the broom from the floor below, which
never failed to make me jump. Outstanding. Man. Excellent.

DEREK MAHON
(b. 1941)

Morning Radio

(for John Scotney)

The silence of the ether . . .
What can be going on
In the art-deco liner?

Ah, now the measured pips,
A stealth of strings
Tickling the fretwork throat,

Woodwinds entering
Delicately, the clarinet
Ascending to a lark-like note.

Seven o'clock –
News-time, and the merciful
Voice of Tom Crowe

Explains with sorrow
That the world we know
Is coming to an end.

Even as he speaks
We can hear furniture
Creak and slide on the decks.

But first a brief recital
Of resonant names –
Mozart, Schubert, Brahms.

The sun shines,
And a new day begins
To the strains of a horn concerto.

ROBERT MINHINNICK
(b. 1952)

Short Wave

I try to tune in, but Europe's blurred voice
Becomes stranger with the movement of the dial.

All stations seem to give a fragment of
Performance, - Mozart disarmed by a fizzled
Prodigy; innumerable cliques of wordsmiths.

As the electric crackles I make believe
I am composing an avant-garde symphony,
A sound poem for a hall of idiot speech.

But behind the static are moments of sanity:
A string quartet and interesting chanteuse,
Then histrionics at a play's climax.

For some reason, a hubbub of languages
And dim music becomes more important
Than any scheduled programme. It suits

My mood perhaps, this indecipherable mayhem
Of newscasters and sopranos, and the long
Returns to electronic gibbering.

Somewhere, behind a rockband's sudden squall,
A morse message is tapped out. For a few seconds
It is clear, articulate, before melting

Into Europe's verbiage. It was not mayday.
And I twist the dial a hairsbreadth into jazz.

W. H. AUDEN & CHRISTOPHER ISHERWOOD
(1907–73 & 1904–86)

From: *The Ascent of F6*

Turn off the wireless.
      Tune in to another station;
To the tricks of variety
      or the rhythm of jazz.
Let us roll back the carpet
      from the parlour floor
And dance to the wireless
      through the open door.

TALK RADIO

V. H. FRIEDLAENDER

Progress

There was a time when peace at evening
Flushed like a flower along the sky
And majesty, on darkening tree-tops,
Went soundless by.

Now, when the sky's a red rose falling,
Switches release on garden dews
Adjacent blarings of loud-speakers,
And substitute, for rapture, news.

ANON.

The News

Some go to lunch at midday,
And some at half past one;
While some for a penny, consume at any
Old time, the egregious bun;
And tea-time may be five-ish,
Or four-ish, as you choose,
But all must agree with this firm decree –
Everything stops for the news.

The Cook throws down her thriller
And Jean, her homework sums,
And Dad takes off his specs, to cough
And arrange his elbows and thumbs:
And Pussy looks up from her washing
And Mum from her crossword clues
And, eyes a-glisten, we settle to listen –
Everything stops for the news.

Radio Times, 1936

BERTOLT BRECHT (trans. John Willett)
(1898–1956)

To My Little Radio

You little box I carried on that trip
Concerned to save your works from getting broken
Fleeing from house to train, from train to ship
So I might hear the hated jargon spoken.
Beside my bedside and to give me pain
Last thing at night, once more as dawn appears
Shouting their victories and my worst fears:
Promise at least you won't go dead again!

GEOFFREY HILL
(b. 1932)

From: *Speech! Speech!*

22

Age of mass consent: go global with her.
Challenge satellite failure, the primal
violent day-star moody as Herod.
Forget nothing. Reprieve no-one. Exempt
only her bloodline's *jus natalium.*
Pledge to immoderacy the outraged
hardly forgiven mourning of the PEOPLE,
inexorable, though in compliance,
media-conjured. Inscrutable Í call
her spirit nów on this island: memory
subsiding into darkness | nowhere
coming to rest.

23

It has its own voice, certainly, though that
fails to come through. Try Hilversum. The Dutch
are heroes | living as they have to. Give
Luxembourg a miss for old times' sake.
Recall the atmospherics. Stoicism
may well serve | fill its own vacancy.
Step forward, you. Speak at the red light.
What else proclaims us? More suggestions please.
Autographed hate-mail preferred. Everything sounds
THE CRY OF THE AFFLICTED. Thát any cause
to delete other options? Talk me thróugh this,
Gallant Little Belgium | I still hear you.

LOUIS ARAGON (trans. Rolfe Humphries)
(1897–1982)

From: *Little Suite for Loudspeaker*

Hilversum, Kalundborg, Brno, the loud world over
Monday to Sunday, the idiot radio
Spits germs on Mozart, dedicates to you
Silence, its endlessly insulting brew

Loud Jove in love with Io, queen of cows
Has left her tethered by the waterside
She hears by radio at eventide
Cracklings of static from the hidden spouse

Like her – for this is war – hearing the Voice
Men stay in their stupidity and caress
Toulouse, PTT, Daventry, Bucharest

Their hope, the good old hope of former days
Interrogates the ether, which replies
That Carter's little liver pills are best.

D. H. LAWRENCE
(1885–1930)

Broadcasting to the G. B. P.

'Hushabye baby, on a tree top
when the wind blows, the cradle shall rock,
when the bough breaks –'

Stop that at once!
You'll give the Great British Public a nervous shock!

'Goosey goosey gander
whither do you wander
upstairs, downstairs
in the lady's –'

Stop! where's your education?
Don't you know that's obscene?
Remember the British Public!

'Baa-baa black sheep
have you any wool?
yes sir! yes sir!
three bags full!
One for the master, and one for the dame,
And one for the little boy that lives down the –'

No! You'd better omit that, too communistic!
Remember the state of mind of the British Public.

'Pussy-cat pussy-cat where have you been?
I've been up to London to see the fine queen!
Pussy-cat pussy-cat what did you there?
I frightened a little mouse –'

       Thank you! thank you!
There are no mice in our Royal Palaces. Omit it!

LEROI JONES (Amiri Baraka)
(b. 1934)

In Memory of Radio

Who has ever stopped to think of the divinity of Lamont Cranston?
(Only Jack Kerouac, that I know of: & me.
The rest of you probably had on WCBS and Kate Smith,
Or something equally unattractive.)

What can I say?
It is better to have loved and lost
Than to put linoleum in your living rooms?

Am I a sage or something?
Mandrake's hypnotic gesture of the week?
(Remember, I do not have the healing powers of Oral Roberts . . .
I cannot, like F. J. Sheen, tell you how to get saved & *rich!*
I cannot even order you to gaschamber satori like Hitler or Goody
      Knight)

& Love is an evil word.
Turn it backwards/see, see what I mean?
An evol word. & besides
who understands it?
I certainly wouldn't like to go out on that kind of limb.

Saturday mornings we listened to the *Red Lantern* & his undersea
      folk.
At 11, *Let's Pretend* & we did/& I, the poet, still do, Thank God!

What was it he used to say (after the transformation when he was
    safe
& invisible & the unbelievers couldn't throw stones?) 'Heh, heh,
    heh.
Who knows what evil lurks in the hearts of men? The Shadow
    knows!'

O, yes he does
O, yes he does
An evil word it is,
This love.

PETER PORTER
(b. 1929)

Radio Caliban

This is Imagination's nuclear-free zone,
so answer, airwaves, answer!
And hello to the girl
who asked for Ariel's new single.

Personally I'd take Wallace Stevens
to Prospero any day, and here's
that smouldering oldie, 'The Bermudas' –
Andy Marvell in the English Boat.

Time now for our popular feature
'My Most Wimpish Moment',
but first let's join Trink and Steff
singing 'I Cried to Dream Again.'

Our Studio Doctor says
women who eat meat grow more body hair –
Remember you heard it first on Radio Caliban,
the voice from the middle of the sandwich.

I saw God in an oleander bush,
writes Mrs Sycorax of Alfred Avenue
and, yes, Miss Mandeville, by starlight
a word may seem a planet. Hang on in.

Don Alonso of Bellosguardo
wants to know what became of
'The Thousand Twangling Instruments' –
same group, Don, I've got them on the brain.

If you don't want worms, lay off the cheese.
When the big wedding's on – Miranda
and Ferdy coming down the aisle –
all eyes are on the bridesmaids' boobs.

Watch an ant drag ten times its weight,
that's your blood holding back your death.
What you write makes sense or else words
would curl up in your palm like a paper fish.

Not much rhythm, not much art –
all right, but it's got feelings, listeners!
So let a lady wrangle with the blues,
'They flee from me that sometime did me seek.'

Absolute Milan where wise savers go.
A great video, those cloud-capped towers,
and Giorgione storming on the shelf –
a coral island ringed by sun and surf.

STELLA DAVIS
(b. 1948)

Friends Beyond

(After Hardy)

Polly Perks and Walter Gabriel, old Dan Archer late at plough,
           Grace and Jack and Ned and Doris
Squire Ralph and Mrs Perkins, lie in Ambridge churchyard now.

'Gone,' I call them, gone for good, that tried and trusted bunch
           And yet at five past seven
Or on Sundays when the meat has just begun to roast for lunch

They've a way of whispering to me, listener who's still around,
           In soft persuasive tones
Like persistent dead leaves rusting as they flutter to the ground:

'We have triumphed: our creation was the best we could achieve,
           And now we do not fail
To root you in a landscape from which we took our leave.

'We are dead, but now you listen to our children who have grown
           To maturity, like yours:
Our families and histories are bound up with your own.

'The views that rolled before us from the brow of Lakey hill
           Are unaltered in your eyes;
Our pastoral contentment is a dream that charms you still.'

Thus with certainty of heaven, and no real fear of hell,
           In their familiar tones,
While I peer into the oven where the meat is browning well,

Polly Perks and Walter Gabriel, old Dan Archer late at plough,
           Grace and Jack and Ned and Doris
Squire Ralph and Mrs Perkins, murmur mildly to me now.

GAVIN EWART
(1916–95)

Radio Cricket

Can't you just see them,
sitting there in the Commentary Box,
drinking tea, passing round the sweets,
eating the big cakes their admirers send them?
Blowers, Fred, Trevor, the Alderman,
The Bearded Wonder?

Prep School boys with nicknames,
sitting there in their shorts,
wearing their little school caps –
wool stockings up to their knees,
with elastic garters!

LOUIS MACNEICE
(1907–63)

From: *Autumn Journal*

And the next day begins
   Again with alarm and anxious
Listening to bulletins
   From distant, measured voices
Arguing for peace
   While the zero hour approaches,
While the eagles gather and the petrol and oil and grease
   Have all been applied and the vultures back the eagles.
But once again
   The crisis is put off and things look better
And we feel negotiation is not vain –
   Save my skin and damn my conscience.
And negotiation wins,
   If you can call it winning,
And here we are – just as before – safe in our skins;
   Glory to God for Munich.
And stocks go up and wrecks
   Are salved and politicians' reputations
Go up like Jack-on-the-Beanstalk; only the Czechs
   Go down and without fighting.

JULIAN MAY
(b. 1955)

On the Air

1.
Moscow is yelling down the line
'. . . the co-operation of Socialism . . .'
Washington bites back, too loud
'. . . Capitalism's diversity . . .'

London reasonably weighs
each consideration,
turning its back, some observers note,
to balance argument.

                    I balance mere sound,
tired of it all –
quotidian surfeit of events
unfit for human consumption,
analysis, comment, the puke of half-chewed news.
Goose-stepping endless information
fires language's gaunt crops.

2.
Once upon a time
the voice of truth calmly announced
'There is no news tonight.'
Now the slots must always be filled,
on the hour, every hour.
So at dawn on this thin Monday
the talking-head reads once more
the bulletin he read all night before.

Then, having a few seconds still to fill,
tells me what I need to know –
it is the first day of spring (official)
but here in London there is heavy rain.
I think how beyond these soundproof walls
its acid digests the stone carvings
of Saint Mary-Le-Strand
and spreads in waves like radio to the Urals
blighting Europe's trees . . .

and miss my cue. Silence,
and the red light glows.
I hit a switch then fade
the sig. to time.
                    Time may come
when again there will be no news:
the producer's recurring nightmare,
dead air, endless dead air.

W. H. AUDEN & CHRISTOPHER ISHERWOOD
(1907–73 & 1904–86)

From: *The Ascent of F6*

Turn off the wireless; we are tired
    of descriptions of travel;
We are bored by the exploits of
    amazing heroes;
We do not wish to be heroes,
    nor are we likely to travel;
We shall not penetrate
    the Arctic Circle . . .

WEATHER

ELEANOR FARJEON
(1881–1965)

F is for Forecast

The farmer with his weather-powers
Can always, within certain hours,
Read England's weather at a glance –
But not the weather out in France.

Behold! the Broadcast Forecast came
To birth! and those who cast the same
Sweep the Horizon news to win
For farmers who are listening-in.

And now the farmer knows what feast
Of sun is coming from the East,
Knows when his furrows will be blessed
With feeding rainfalls from the West;

He from the Forecast now will know
When broadcast he his seeds may sow,
When it is wise to cut his hay,
And when to cart the corn away.

SEAMUS HEANEY
(b. 1939)

From: *Glanmore Sonnets*

Dogger, Rockall, Malin, Irish Sea:
Green, swift upsurges, North Atlantic flux
Conjured by that strong gale-warning voice,
Collapse into a sibilant penumbra.
Midnight and closedown. Sirens of the tundra,
Of eel-road, seal-road, keel-road, whale-road, raise
Their wind-compounded keen behind the baize
And drive the trawlers to the lee of Wicklow.
L'Etoile, Le Guillemot, La Belle Hélène
Nursed their bright names this morning in the bay
That toiled like mortar. It was marvellous
And actual, I said out loud, 'A haven,'
The word deepening, clearing, like the sky
Elsewhere on Minches, Cromarty, The Faroes.

SEÁN STREET
(b. 1946)

Shipping Forecast, Donegal

They have shared still late October,
but salt stones and a broken tree,
the peeled paint on the lifeboat house
chime with places where the glass falls,
prime sources encountering night's bald predications.

Everywhere winter edges in,
and now the time is ten to six . . .

lightness and weight, air's potentials
pressed into words, implication;
here – on all coasts – listening grows passionately tense.

Fair Isle, Faeroes, South East Iceland,
North Utsire, South Utsire,
Fisher, German Bight, Tyne, Dogger . . .
This pattern of names on the sea –
weather's unlistening geography – paves water.
Beyond the music, the singing
of sounds – this minimal chanting,
this ritual pared to the bone
becomes the cold poetry of information.

The litany edges closer –
Lundy, Fastnet and Irish Sea . . .
Routine enough, all just routine.
Always his eyes guessing beyond
the headland, she perhaps sleeping, no words spoken.

He stretches forward to grasp it,
claims his radio place – *and now*
the weather reports from coastal stations
and then: *Malin Head* – such routine
that she barely glances up, but hears *now falling.*

CAROL ANN DUFFY
(b. 1955)

Prayer

Some days, although we cannot pray, a prayer
utters itself. So, a woman will lift
her head from the sieve of her hands and stare
at the minims sung by a tree, a sudden gift.

Some nights, although we are faithless, the truth
enters our hearts, that small familiar pain;
then a man will stand stock-still, hearing his youth
in the distant Latin chanting of a train.

Pray for us now. Grade 1 piano scales
console the lodger looking out across
a Midlands town. Then dusk, and someone calls
a child's name as though they named their loss.

Darkness outside. Inside, the radio's prayer –
Rockall. Malin. Dogger. Finisterre.

DUNCAN FORBES
(b. 1947)

Forecast

A woman's voice is reading out
The forecast in a studio,
Dogger, Fisher, German Bight,
And listening to the radio
A mother knits a jersey of
Colours you could paint a boat:
Green, pink, turquoise, purple, blue.
A row of russet on the cuff –
Humber, Thames, Dover, Wight –
And soon it should be finished off
North 5 or 6, winds, variable.
Unlike the fleeces of Fastnet,
The underbelly loops of wool
Look colourful and comfortable,
Miles from the ships at sea tonight
In *Portland, Plymouth, Lundy, Sole.*

IN THE CAR

DANA GIOIA
(b. 1950)

Cruising with the Beach Boys

So strange to hear that song again tonight
Travelling on business in a rented car
Miles from anywhere I've been before.
And now a tune I haven't heard for years,
Probably not since it last left the charts
Back in LA in 1969.
I can't believe I know the words by heart
And can't think of a girl to blame them on.

Every lovesick summer has its song,
And this one I pretended to despise,
But if I was alone when it came on,
I turned it up full-blast to sing along –
A primal scream in croaky baritone,
The notes all flat, the lyrics mostly slurred.
No wonder I spent so much time alone
Making the rounds in Dad's old Thunderbird.

Some nights I drove down to the beach to park
And walk along the railings of the pier.
The water down below was cold and dark,
The waves monotonous against the shore.
The darkness and the mist, the midnight sea,
The flickering lights reflected from the city –
A perfect setting for a boy like me,
The Cecil B. DeMille of my self-pity.

I thought by now I'd left those nights behind,
Lost like the girls that I never could get,
Gone with the years, junked with the old T-Bird.
But one old song, a stretch of empty road,
Can open up a door and let them fall
Tumbling like boxes from a dusty shelf,
Tightening my throat for no reason at all
Bringing on tears shed only for myself.

DEIRDRE SHANAHAN
(b. 1955)

Morning Radio

I knit a way through the traffic,
along Holborn, Cheapside, past the Banks
as Henry Blofeld reports from Faisalabad
on the morning radio.

White sleeves flash in the heat of Lahore
but I am aged eight, at home,
lost to the lawn, playing
at countries, people, ages.

A whirr of ball, a strike
and clapping rolls
as leather traps a long arm of wood
in the breeze.

An imperative thud
filters through trees.
The cricketers are out and eskimoed
and the scoreboard sails again.

MARTYN CRUCEFIX
(b. 1956)

Air-Waves

As I slowed up and shifted down gear,
a dance song thumping from the car radio
was stretched out and smashed to pieces.

But we barely noticed that first time –
all eager to see the house, where it stood
beneath the surfing crackle of the pylons.

The girls loved the sight of so much sky.
They slipped into new schools with ease
though Sue and I made it home more slowly.

And by then, there was Stephen, almost four,
suddenly ill, his rush of growing gone awry,
and the doctor's face, closed up and dark

as the Manchester streets we had left behind.
He could tell me nothing. Inexplicable,
the pattern of disease. *A year – maybe two.*

Driving back across the hills, roadside wires
loop down, are yanked back to the blunted head
of each telegraph pole – and further off,

the pylons, hitching up skeins of darkness,
striding up country to a house where this car
and their sheaf of hot wires converge,

where a young man's voice on the radio
will melt down in a surge of boiling static
as I slow up, shift gear, and stop.

JOHN POWELL WARD
(b. 1937)

Eros

23 April 1995

Valley of the Usk, exactly mid-distant
From the road; beautifully wrapped in its fields;
Sheep like bees in the evening. Mazy light.
The Usk is surprisingly deep by Llansantffraed
Bridge, where its water swivels round the pilings.
On the lush meadow cows munched heavily.
I left at dusk for the four-hour slog.

Piccadilly. Midnight radio: 'A new biography
Of Henry Vaughan . . . tell us about him, here
On his hillside.' Squads of neon march overhead.
In the middle, on a stone knoll, love's statue
Opens its wings but never flies, the perennial
Bush for town foxes. To wheel us forward,
A glade of traffic lights, each with its green leaf.

ANTONY DUNN
(b. 1973)

Radio

What sounds like the broadcast of snow itself
among mountains visible only by
the absence of stars, is the radio's
wheezing stagger between its lost stations.

Half an hour of the sky's current affairs
murmur in the back of the car
as we order orange digits this way
and that in the dashboard's familiar dark;

until a voice stags the black-white airwaves.
She announces herself like the smell of
cocoa, or of grandparents' bed-linen,
Turns the radio's display to a hearth.

Aunty Jean, anachronist in-between
the songs of her Sunday night music-show,
talks us through unguessable lochs and drops
of this road through the highlands, and the snow

mothing our headlights. Outside this warm space
untold deer, in their camouflage, adjust
their antenna to the white-noised engine,
deaf to the one broadcast passing through them.

She's not really called Aunty Jean, she says,
as the radio loses her,
and the dark air empties itself again
of everything but darkness and the snow.

LISTENERS

THE WESTERN BROTHERS

From: *We're Frightfully BBC*

(Popular recording, 1935)

Connected with County, and landed estates,
We *never* cross cutlery over our plates;
We crawl to the City, perhaps Mincing Lane
And potter to luncheon, and crawl home again.
We're really too rugger and soccer,
Too painfully quick off the tee,
We pile all our togs in a locker,
Our sweaters have quite a low V.
We know the announcers and Greenwich pip-pips,
We simply *adore* the gale warnings to ships,
We *never* pour vinegar over our chips –
We're frightfully BBC.

RICHARD CHURCH
(1893–1972)

Earphones

Sounds came sifting down
As I fastened the phones.
Music crowned the cottage.
The trees outside
Wrung their hands and cried in vain,
Unheard, forgotten . . .
No latch clicked,
Nor door rattled,
Nor ivy at window tapped,
For I was far away,
Listening to the great orchestra
Bowing and drumming
In Germany.

RONALD FRANKAU
(1894–1951)

Thoughts While Broadcasting

(Dedicated to a Studio Audience)

Pity the man who stands alone
Before the wretched microphone,
And visions, as I often do,
The millions that he's talking to –
While those who're in the studio
Look at him, but cannot know
How much poor folk like I depend
Upon the clapping at the end,
Which gives the hidden audience ground
To think I'm better than I sound.

I see them all – that hidden crowd,
Soft listeners with their speakers loud.
I see the honest – and the few
Whose licences are overdue.
I see that nasty man in Gough
Who, when I started, switched me off –
That Peckham lady on a diet
Who says 'Oh, 'Erbert, do keep quiet.
I want to 'ear Jack 'Ulbert, dear.'
I see the Moderns of Mayfair
Who say, 'This Vaudeville's a sin.
Get Paris, Tom, or try Berlin.'
While in the North my smartest shaft
Is greeted with 'This fellow's daft.
Leon Henry is *my* choice of wags,
For I can oonderstand '*is* gags.'

While up in Scotland I could bet
Says one, who owns a home-made set,
'Wha's this fellow trying to tell?
I dinna think he knows his-sel'.'
I see in Ireland, Tims and Pats
Murmur, as they grab their hats,
'This isn't very good oi think,
Let's go out and have a dhrink.'
Some Davies says in Celtic tones,
'Indeed to goodness, Owen Jones,
I hear good music when I can,
Let's get on to Cardiff, man.'

Those others, too, I fearfully see,
The fans who think a lot of me.
Do *they* say now, as I recite,
'He isn't half as good tonight'?
(Though hard to earn a fame for wit
The real job is in keeping it.)
I tremble, too, as here I stand,
To think the *great ones* of the land
May listen with a sapient frown
To this bald, broadcasting clown –
Lords Beaverbrook and Rothermere,
MacDonald, Archibald de Bear,
Baldwin, Lloyd George, Eva Moore,
Malcolm Campbell, Bernard Shaw . . . .
Does my voice attract Miss El'nor Glyn?
Is C. B. Cochran listening in?
Who knows how names may soon be smudged
By a broadcast badly judged?

I fear the order's far too tall!
I can't succeed in pleasing all.
So pity the man who stands alone

Before the wretched microphone,
And, for a fee of medium size,
Is not allowed to advertise,
Nor say a word which might offend.
But nebulously must depend
Upon a humour frightfully chaste –
And yet appeal to *every* taste.

Enough! I've really got to go.
Do clap me in the studio.
Listeners then are really bound
To think I'm better than I sound.
So give us, please, your kind applause.
You're safe – we never give encores.

What the Listener Thinks

'What the other listener thinks';
A page where listeners air their kinks;
Where colonels grouse and rip and roar
And maiden aunts lay down the law.

Now if I were the BBC,
And had such letters sent to me,
I shouldn't worry what to do –
Please the many or anger the few . . .

But for each and every item
That people wrote, who didn't like 'em,
From the programme I would strike 'em.
Oh! I'm sure that I'd delight 'em.

I'd drop light and classic music
Talks and concerts I'd delete,
And on the ether golden silence
Then would reign as king complete.

Radio Times, 1931

DAVID GASCOYNE
(1916–2001)

The Nightwatchers

Let those who hear this voice become aware
The sun has set. O night-time listeners,
You sit in lighted rooms marooned by darkness,
And through dark ether comes a voice to bid you
All be reminded that the night surrounds you.

...

Let those who hear my voice become aware
That Night has fallen. We are in the dark.
I do not see you, but in my mind's eye
You sit in lighted rooms marooned by darkness.
My message is sent out upon the waves
Of a black boundless sea to where you drift,
Each in a separate lit room, as though on rafts,
Survivors of the great lost ship, *The Day.*

Let those who hear our voices be aware
That Night now reigns on earth. Nocturnal listeners,
The time you hear me in is one of darkness,
And round us, as within us, battle rages . . .

From *Night Thoughts*

EDWARD STOREY
(b. 1930)

The Wireless Aerial

(for David Twigg)

Twice as high as the clothes-line,
it went from pole to pole like rigging
over the deck of our garden.

Because of it we could hear people
speaking in London and Big Ben tolling
silence for the evening news.

There wasn't much that aerial couldn't do –
music, plays and comedians filled up the house
like favourite relatives.

How words which were invisible
came through the air to drop the world
right on our doorstep puzzled me.

But pole to pole was nearer to the truth
than we perceived. One Sunday morning
came the thin dry voice of Neville Chamberlain.

We sat in autumn stillness round the room
as mourners waiting for a funeral.
I felt our aerial had let us down.

Yet what I now remember most
is not the war, the sirens, or the bombs,
but how a blackbird always sang

from the tall and rough-hewn mast
high as our roof, its notes vibrating
in a clear blue glass of sky.

He and the blossom on the garden wall
became a well of indescribable delight
from which those echoes now return.

And nothing can destroy that world
though words remain as difficult to find
as wavelengths lost among the stars.

GEORGE GROSSMITH & P. G. WODEHOUSE
(1847–1912 & 1881–1975)

You Can't Make Love by Wireless

(Song lyric, 1923)

You can't make love by wireless;
It's like bread without the jam.
There's nothing girls desire less
Than a cold Marconigram
For it's something you can't speak to
From a someone you can't see
It's like a village church that's spireless
Or a little home that's fireless
Or a motor car that's tyre-less
(Or a Selfridge's that's buyer-less)
And it isn't any good to me.

TODD SWIFT
(b. 1966)

My Radios

My radios came at all hours, on different days.
Sometimes they were my father, dressed down
for baseball, on his bed, and all was good;
then there was 'Father Robert Johnson', crazed

with The Lord, whose call-in shows were doomed
with late-night suicides and talk of Sodom's sins;
then, the house dark, that man's gilded voice
spent its charity on emptiness; my father snored.

I lay awake until the morning news, and dawn,
amazed that the end was upon us, none spared
except the ones who took Him into their souls,
then got up to sassy jingles for designer jeans,
and snowstorms, which some weeks God sent.

GEORGE SZIRTES
(b. 1948)

Short Wave

1.

Somewhere in there, in a gap between a taxi
and some indecipherable station
there is a frequency that's unfrequented
like an island, an administration
of ethereal incompetence, the voice of Caliban
deserted but with remnants of quaint speech,
an accent or two that could be out of Shakespeare.

You tune in but the voice is out of reach
and seems merely to flirt with meaning; dry trees
rattling on an unprotected hillside,
hollow tubes wind whistles through. It speaks
at length through a protracted landslide.

Whoever lives here the transmitting tower
is out of date, there is no programme schedule
to list what may be listened to, what hour
the one clear and intelligible accent
will burst like a soprano voice along
the curving sea between the taxi, France
and Germany, all Europe in her song.

2.

This landscape is eternal night − not hell
or purgatory, just a weave of streets
settling like a cobweb late at night
in greys and greens, advances and retreats.

Only drunkards reel home, slam the door
and wander over to the wireless
to turn the dial in hope of finding music,
celestial and perfect more or less.

3.
These reasonable voices going on
and on, unconscionably long
at all hours of the day and night
mean nothing in most places, not to me.
I speak no Dutch or Spanish, tell the truth
I only know my native tongue and French
and that barely sufficient to get by with.

My lips are sour with lager and my head
has no room for a second studio.
Anyway, what do they mean, these voices?
What are they saying? Well, it can be guessed.
Which is why I sit here listening
and turning dials, eavesdropping
on that Balkan baritone
who tells me what the world believes of me.

4.
The planets click like doors or whistle wide.
Their secret messages are understood
by fascinated children in their beds
who're used to lack of sleep and solitude.
Downstairs the broken speech of moving objects
where unrestricted chaos rules the air
and mother is no different from a chair.

We leave the children sleeping and ourselves
lie reading and half listening until
the close-down, when we kiss and frontiers blur

in line with international good will.
There are so many stations on the line,
and other music wells up in the drought
in waves that cancel one another out.

EPILOGUE

CHARLES TOMLINSON
(b. 1927)

In the Studio

'Recorded ambience' – this
is what they call
silences put back
between the sounds:
leaves might fall
on to the roof-glass to compound
an instant ambience
from the drift of sibilants:
but winter boughs
cannot enter – they
distort like weed
under the glass water:
this (sifted) silence
now recording (one
minute only of it)
comprises what
you did not hear before
you began to listen –
the sighs that
in a giant building
rise up trapped between
its sound-proofed surfaces
murmuring, replying
to themselves, gathering
power like static
from the atmosphere: you do
hear this ambience?
it rings true: for silence
is an imagined thing.

ACKNOWLEDGEMENTS

I am grateful to a number of people who helped me in my exploration of the poetry of radio. Firstly my thanks to Jenny Abramsky for her kind opening remarks. Thanks too, to Helen Boaden, Tom Durham, Paul Green, Stephen J. Hackett, Jeremy Nicholas and Colin Thornton who were generous with suggestions and advice while I was on my quest for poems. Likewise my thanks go to the poets who contributed work to the collection: Charles Bennett ('The Drowned Radio'), Keith Bennett ('99.9 FM Radio Nostalgia'), Stella Davis ('Friends Beyond'), Ethan Gilsdorf ('Away From Us'), Desmond Graham ('The Wireless'), James Priory ('Emma and the Radio'), John Powell Ward ('Eros'), and Jonathan Wonham ('Emergency Services'). Dana Gioia allowed me to include 'Cruising with the Beach Boys' from his collection *Daily Horoscope* (Graywolf Press) and Peter Porter kindly granted permission for 'Radio Caliban' (*The Automatic Oracle*, Oxford University Press). Anne Harvey gave permission to include one of Eleanor Farjeon's delightful Radio Alphabet poems, 'F is for Forecast'. Brian Levison's 'Eighth Symphony Interruptus' is taken from *Strange Smells of a Cat* (Redbeck Press) and 'The Wireless Aerial' by Edward Storey comes from his Rockingham Press collection, *A Change in the Climate*. 'Little Suite for Loudspeaker' by Louis Aragon, translated by Rolfe Humphries, is from *Aragon: Poet of Resurgent France*, edited by Hannah Josephson and Malcolm Cowley (Pilot Press). 'Prayer' is taken from *Mean Time* by Carol Ann Duffy, published by Anvil Press Poetry in 1993. 'In Memory of Radio' by LeRoi Jones is taken from *New American Poetry 1945–60*, edited by Donald Allen (Grove Press). Extracts from 'The Ascent of F6' by W. H. Auden and Christopher Isherwood, Seamus Heaney's 'Sonnet VII' from 'Glanmore Sonnets' (*Field Work)* and 'Broadcast' from *Collected Poems* by Philip Larkin are included with the permission of Faber and Faber. Thanks to The Penguin Group for permission to reproduce the extract from *Speech! Speech!* by Geoffrey Hill (Viking), to The Gallery Press and Derek Mahon for 'Morning Radio' from *Collected Poems* and to Peterloo Poets for 'Radio 3' by Brian Waltham from *Music for Brass* and 'On the Air' by Julian May, from *The Earliest Memory*. Gillian Clarke's 'On Air' is taken from *Collected Poems*, Antony Dunn's 'Radio' comes from his collection, *Flying Fish*, 'Short Wave' by Robert Minhinnick is from *Selected Poems* and 'In the Studio' from *The Shaft* by Charles Tomlinson; all are included by permission of Carcanet Press Ltd. 'Wireless' is from *Raising Sparks* by Michael Symmons Roberts, published by Jonathan Cape, and 'Short Wave' by George Szirtes from *Short Wave*, published by Secker and Warburg. Both these poems are used by permission of The Random House Group Ltd. My thanks to Enitharmon Press for the following: the extract from David Gascoyne's great radio poem 'Night Thoughts', from *Selected Poems*; 'Air-Waves' by Martyn Crucefix, from *Beneath Tremendous Rain*; 'Forecast' by Duncan Forbes, from *Public and Confidential*; and 'Morning Radio' by Deirdre Shanahan, from *Legal Tender*. Acknowledgements are also due to the following: the executors of Gavin Ewart for 'Radio Cricket', from *Penultimate Poems* (Hutchinson), David Higham Associates for the extract from 'Autumn Journal' from *Collected Poems* by Louis MacNeice (Faber), The Society of Authors as the Literary Representatives of the Estate of Alfred Noyes for permission to include 'The Dane Tree'. Every reasonable attempt has been made to trace the copyright holders of the poems collected in this volume; apologies are tendered for any omissions or errors, which will be corrected in subsequent editions.